Polar Bears

Polar Bears

Go Facts
Polar Bears
ISBN: 1-86509-312-2

Copyright © 2004 Blake Publishing

Published in the UK by Badger Publishing Limited
Oldmedow Road, Hardwick Industrial Estate, King's Lynn PE30 4JJ
Telephone: 01438 791037
www.badgerlearning.co.uk

2 4 6 8 10 9 7 5 3 1

© BLAKE PUBLISHING
This edition is for sale in the UK and EU only

Written by Katy Pike
Publisher: Katy Pike
Editors: Maureen O'Keefe and Garda Turner
Design and layout by The Modern Art Production Group
Photo research by Tracey Gibson
Photos by John Foxx, Photodisc, Brand X, Corbis, Image 100, Comstock, Digital Vision, Goodshoot, Image State, Inmagine, Art Today and Thinkstock
Printed in the UK by Zoom Digital Print Limited

This publication is copyright ©. No part of this book may be reproduced by any means without written permission from the publisher.

Contents

4   Studying Polar Bears

8   Find and Watch

12   How Heavy?

14   How Many Cubs?

Studying Polar Bears

Scientists study polar bears to find out more about them. They ask questions. What questions would you like to ask about polar bears?

Here are some questions.
How heavy are polar bears?
How many **cubs** in a **litter**?
How long do the cubs stay with their mother?

Scientists can study polar bears from a distance.

Scientists use **binoculars** and telescopes. They record what they see on video and with cameras.

A scientist needs:

✓ binoculars

✓ telescope

✓ camera

✓ video camera.

Find and Watch

How to find a polar bear

1. Find some polar bear tracks in the snow.
2. Follow the footprints.
3. Don't get too close. Polar bears can be dangerous.

Polar bears make large tracks in the snow.

How to watch a polar bear

1 Use a safe, strong vehicle.

2 Drive to where the polar bears live.

3 Watch the bears and see what they do. Maybe the bears will watch you too.

Polar bears are interested in people.

How Heavy?

How to weigh a polar bear

1 Put the bear to sleep with a special **dart**.

2 Place a net around the polar bear.

3 Lift and weigh the bear. Polar bears are very large, heavy animals.

Polar bears can weigh 600 kilograms.

How Many Cubs?

How many cubs in a litter of polar bears?

① Look for polar bears with cubs.

② Count the number of cubs.

③ Record your results. Some cubs are small and others are almost as big as their mother.

Cubs stay with their mother for more than two years.

Glossary

binoculars special glasses to help you see far away

cubs baby bears

dart a small, sharp arrow

litter baby animals all born together

Index

binoculars 6

camera 6

cubs 5, 14

litter 5, 14

scientist 4, 6

tracks 8